PROFIT
WITHOUT
APOLOGY

ONKAR GHATE
AND DON WATKINS

PROFIT
WITHOUT
APOLOGY

THE NEED TO STAND UP FOR BUSINESS

ARU PRESS

ARU 📖 PRESS

Copyright © 2025 by The Ayn Rand® Institute
All rights reserved.

ISBN: 978-0-9794661-0-6

Cover by Jesse Hashagen
Design by George L. Tibbitts

aynrand.org

Contents

Introduction	1
Profit Without Apology: The Need to Stand Up for Business	9
Open Letter to Sundar Pichai and the Google Team	31
Standing Up to DEI Activism: A Guide for Executives	39
Atlas Shrugged: America's Second Declaration of Independence	67
Endnotes	100
About the Contributors	106
About the Ayn Rand Institute	107

INTRODUCTION

"I refuse to apologize for my ability—I refuse to apologize for my success—I refuse to apologize for my money. If this is evil, make the most of it."

⌒

THIS BOOK IS A CALL TO ARMS for an embattled group of heroes widely seen as villains: productive businessmen. They are exemplars of the American ideal of the pursuit of happiness, responsible for the unprecedented progress and prosperity of our world, but unjustly condemned as greedy exploiters. Why?

"As a group, businessmen have been withdrawing for decades from the ideological battlefield," Ayn Rand observed in 1971. "Their public policy has consisted in appeasing, compromising and apologizing: appeasing their crudest, loudest antagonists;

compromising with any attack, any lie, any insult; apologizing for their own existence."

This withdrawal has helped create a world saturated with anti-business ideas, which businessmen unwittingly enable. The first essay in this collection, "Profit Without Apology," argues that the deepest roots of that anti-business prejudice are found in today's prevailing moral viewpoint, which Rand terms the ethics of altruism. This essay serves as a kind of manifesto for The Atlas Circle, an initiative of the Ayn Rand Institute created to stand up for business—and to empower business leaders to stand up for themselves.

We chose the name "Atlas Circle" because the initiative is rooted in Rand's revolutionary philosophy of Objectivism, dramatized in her bestselling novel *Atlas Shrugged*. That book is an ode to productive businessmen, which they so richly deserved but never before received. More deeply, that book, I argue in "*Atlas Shrugged*: America's Second Declaration of Independence," provides the moral foundation that America's political system needed. The Founding Fathers championed the individual's pursuit of happiness but never offered an account of why this is in fact the moral ideal. Consequently, the Founders' political vision was replaced with one aligned not with the individual's pursuit of happiness but with the individual's self-sacrificial service to the public good. Rand's philosophic work fulfills the Founders' project.

The next two essays apply Rand's philosophic ideas to expose and to counter attacks on business. They are examples of the work we are doing through the Atlas Circle initiative.

"An Open Letter to Sundar Pichai and the Google Team" argues that the antitrust case against Google is predicated not on any actual wrongdoing, but on the company's earned success. Google is being persecuted precisely for its virtues. In this open letter, ARI takes a public stand to expose that profound injustice.

"Standing Up to DEI Activism: A Guide for Executives" offers practical guidance for business leaders who want to resist the pressure to implement Diversity, Equity, and Inclusion (DEI) policies in their companies. That advice, framed by Rand's philosophy, is grounded in a distinctively American individualism.

The spirit that animates this book—and the Atlas Circle's wider work to encourage businessmen to stand up for their own moral right to produce, trade and profit—is best captured in a powerful passage from *Atlas Shrugged*. In this scene, Hank Rearden, a pioneering steel industrialist, speaks at his own trial for violating government rationing of a metal alloy that he invented.

Rearden's courtroom statement is a declaration of moral independence for the American businessman, a refusal to apologize for success, and a celebration of the producer's virtues. His words, which deserve to be quoted at length, exhibit a self-esteem and courage that will be necessary from businessmen today to win their freedom and their right to the pursuit of happiness.

> I do not want my attitude to be misunderstood. I shall be glad to state it for the record. . . . I work for nothing but my own profit—which I make by selling a product they need to men who are willing and able to buy it. I do not produce it for their benefit at the expense of mine, and they do not buy it for my benefit at the expense of theirs; I do not sacrifice my interests to them nor do they sacrifice theirs to me; we deal as equals by mutual consent to mutual advantage—and I am proud of every penny that I have earned in this manner. I am rich and I am proud of every penny I own. I made my money

by my own effort, in free exchange and through the voluntary consent of every man I dealt with—the voluntary consent of those who employed me when I started, the voluntary consent of those who work for me now, the voluntary consent of those who buy my product. I shall answer all the questions you are afraid to ask me openly. Do I wish to pay my workers more than their services are worth to me? I do not. Do I wish to sell my product for less than my customers are willing to pay me? I do not. Do I wish to sell it at a loss or give it away? I do not. If this is evil, do whatever you please about me, according to whatever standards you hold. These are mine. I am earning my own living, as every honest man must. I refuse to accept as guilt the fact of my own existence and the fact that I must work in order to support it. I refuse to accept as guilt the fact that I am able to do it and do it well. I refuse to accept as guilt the fact that I am able to do it better than most people—the fact that my work is of greater value than the work of my neighbors and that more men are willing to pay me. I refuse to apologize for my ability—I refuse to apologize for my success—I refuse to apologize for my money. If this is evil, make the most of it. If this is what the public finds harmful to its interests, let the public destroy me. This is my code—and I will accept no other. I could say to you that I have done more good for my fellow men than you can ever hope to accomplish—but I will not say it, because I do not seek the good of others as a sanction for my right to exist, nor do I recognize the good of others as a justification for their seizure of my property or their destruction of my life. I will not say that the good of others was the purpose of my work—my own good was my purpose, and I despise the man who surrenders his. I could say to you that you do not serve the public good—that nobody's good can be achieved at the price of human sacrifices—that when you violate the rights of one man, you have violated the rights of all, and a public of rightless creatures is doomed to destruction. I could say to you that you will and can achieve nothing but universal devastation—as any looter must, when he runs out of victims. I could say it, but I won't. It is not your particular policy that I challenge, but your moral premise. If it were true that men could achieve their good by means of turning some men into sacrificial animals, and I were asked to immolate myself for the sake of creatures who wanted to survive at the price of my blood, if I were asked to serve the interests of society apart from, above and against my own—I would refuse. I would reject it as the most contemptible evil, I would fight it with every power I possess, I would fight the whole of mankind, if one minute were all I could last before I were murdered, I would fight in the full confidence of the justice of my battle and of a living being's right to exist. Let there be no misunderstanding about me. If it is now the belief of my fellow men, who call themselves the public, that their good requires victims, then I say: The public good be damned, I will have no part of it!

It is precisely *this* attitude of moral self-confidence that we seek to enable and encourage in business leaders. Equipped with the right ideas, the power of their voice is far greater than they realize.

Of course, there are risks in speaking up. But the price of appeasing one's enemies and apologizing for one's virtues is defeat.

Onkar Ghate

PROFIT WITHOUT APOLOGY
The Need to Stand Up for Business

Don Watkins

BUSINESSMEN ARE GUILTY OF A MORAL CRIME. Their crime is not that they've manipulated, defrauded, or exploited humanity. As a group, they are responsible for creating the world of abundance that has lifted most of mankind out of poverty and increased lifespans from 30 to 80. No, their crime is that they've been too timid, too apologetic, too hesitant to declare that what they do is *good*.

In a world that treats business as guilty until proven innocent and insists that successful businessmen have a moral obligation to "give something back" (as if they had taken something rather than created something), businessmen have not spoken out in their own defense. They have not said that business is a noble calling, demanding our highest virtues and worthy of our deepest admiration. They have not said that the profit motive fueling their achievements is honorable and that the profits they earn are deserved. They have not insisted on their moral right to freedom from government interference and control.

Instead, businessmen have responded to charges that they are greedy and exploitative with silence—or, worse, by trying to appease their attackers with assurances that their goal is not their own profit but some "social" goal like creating jobs, or paying taxes, or pursuing philanthropy. One way or another, they concede that the core activity of business—seeking profits through production and trade—is dangerous and immoral, and that the moral high ground belongs to the blowhards trying to shame and shackle them.

"As a group," Ayn Rand observed in 1971, "businessmen have been withdrawing for decades from the ideological battlefield, . . . Their public policy has consisted in appeasing, compromising and apologizing: appeasing their crudest, loudest antagonists; compromising with any attack, any lie, any insult; apologizing for their own existence."[1]

Is it any wonder, then, that the public distrusts business and welcomes the regulatory state? If businessmen themselves will not speak out in their own defense, can the public be blamed for thinking it's because the critics are right and there is something sordid about the work and fortunes of businessmen?

It's time that businessmen stop apologizing for their success and start demanding moral recognition for their achievements—and the moral right to their own freedom.

That's why we created the Atlas Circle: to stand up for business and empower businessmen to stand up for themselves. We believe that the work of business is morally good. We believe that businessmen have been singled out for special attack: they are damned precisely for their virtues. And we believe that only by exposing and repudiating the ideas that fuel anti-business sentiment is it possible for businessmen to gain the recognition and freedom they deserve.

Who Moves the World?

We live in an era of incredible progress. Individuals in the advanced world are living longer, healthier, safer, wealthier lives than at any time in history. Not only has life expectancy at birth nearly tripled since the pre-industrial era, but life expectancy at age 50 has risen between five and ten years since 1950.[2] Deaths from accidents—car accidents, plane crashes, falls, fires, drownings—have all plunged by orders of magnitude over the last century.[3] Deaths from climate-related causes, such as drought and storms, have declined by an astonishing 98 percent.[4] On the whole, global prosperity has risen from $3 a day in 1600 to $33 a day, with individuals in the freest countries living on $100 a day—a 30-fold increase.[5]

We take progress for granted, but we shouldn't. Progress is not a given. For most of history, the bulk of humanity lived at the edge of starvation, and economic growth was measured in centuries, not years. That changed around 1800. Why? Because it was only then, with the birth of capitalism, that a new figure entered the historical scene: *the businessman*. He sought to profit by constantly finding new and better ways of doing things. Inventors, innovators, and industrialists pioneered technologies and entire industries that transformed every aspect of human life.

The Energy Revolution. Energy empowers human beings to use machines to do our work for us. It was businessmen like Newcomen and Rockefeller who discovered how to produce low-cost energy to power those machines, creating the fossil fuel industry and unleashing dramatic improvements in every other area of human life.

The Transportation Revolution. For most of human history, human beings could travel no faster than a horse. Businessmen created steam ships, locomotives, cars, and airplanes to close the gap between distance and time. Thanks to entrepreneurs and inventors like Vanderbilt, Ford, and the Wright Brothers, we could move goods and ourselves further, faster, and at lower cost.

The Food Revolution. Throughout history, producing food has been mankind's greatest concern and struggle. But thanks to businessmen, food has never been more abundant, convenient, diverse, or affordable. Because of innovations in agricultural technology, transportation, and refrigeration, fewer agricultural workers than ever grow more food than ever at a lower cost than ever.

The Communication Revolution. Human beings survive by discovering and deploying knowledge. The more knowledge we can access and the faster we can access it, the more we can thrive. A long line of businessmen, from Bell and Edison to Gates and Jobs, brought us the telegraph, the telephone, the radio, the television, the personal computer, the internet, and the smartphones that have made virtually the whole of human knowledge available to us at the touch of a button.

The Health Revolution. Modern medicine gives us more years in our life and more life in our years. Business supplies our doctors and hospitals with MRI machines, pharmaceutical treatments, life-saving stents, and non-invasive surgery technologies that save and improve lives.

The Financial Revolution. Progress is only possible in a world that runs on money, and the financial industry helps deploy money profitably. Venture capitalists, private equity firms, and community banks help spark new ventures and revive failing ones by matching money and talent. They help us mitigate risk through insurance. They help us maximize our consumption through credit cards and other consumer loans. They help us live securely in retirement through low-cost index funds and financial planning services.

We can point to problems and challenges in all of these industries. Every technology and new line of business introduces new risks and challenges. But car accidents don't erase the value of cars. Air pollution doesn't erase the value of low-cost energy. New achievements give rise to new problems for human ingenuity to solve. Progress involves the continual improvement in our ability to meet life's challenges, including the challenges progress itself creates.

But at every step, the individuals driving human life forward are businessmen. Businessmen prosper by translating knowledge into wealth. The sciences expand the frontiers of knowledge, but it is businessmen who figure out how to use that knowledge profitably, how to create the products and services that we use to pursue our happiness. Scientists study energy—businessmen produce the power that runs our factories, farms, homes, and cars. Scientists study diseases—businessmen produce the instruments and drugs that cure disease and improve our quality of life. The businessman, Rand concludes,

> is the great liberator who, in the short span of a century and a half, has released men from bondage to their physical needs, has released them from the terrible drudgery of an eighteen-hour workday of manual labor for their barest subsistence, has released them from famines, from pestilences, from the stagnant hopelessness and terror in which most of mankind had lived in all the pre-capitalist centuries—and in which most of it still lives, in non-capitalist countries.[6]

Value creation is primarily intellectual, and here businessmen make an unmatched contribution. Their *intellectual labor* determines whether a worker produces ten outfits a day or ten thousand—a pencil or a computer—snake oil or a life-saving pharmaceutical. It is businessmen who introduce new products, new services, new tools, new methods of production. It is businessmen who formulate business strategies, and pivot when those strategies fail. It is businessmen who decide who to hire, who to fire, what prices to charge, and how a product should be sold. It is businessmen who risk their life savings and work for years without pay, with nothing but their conviction that the doubters are wrong and that success is possible. All of that takes thought, judgment, and courage. And it is through that intellectual effort that businessmen supply us with the knowledge, resources, and processes that lift our productive power to increasingly greater heights.

If you knew nothing else but that business drives progress, you would assume that it was the most heralded, celebrated profession on earth. The reality is far different.

Our Anti-Business Culture

We live in an anti-business culture. While we will sometimes celebrate top businessmen for their achievements, we nevertheless view them with an air of suspicion and categorically deny them any *moral* recognition for their work.

Even our most successful, most respected business leaders are told they have a moral duty to "give something back." We do not chastise successful scientists, artists, athletes, or even literal lottery winners about "giving back." But to succeed at business is to "take something from society," in Salesforce co-CEO Marc Benioff's words, and the solution is for businessmen to "truly give back and have a positive impact."[7]

This is actually the least negative way successful businessmen are described. The nineteenth-century industrialists who created the modern world were unjustly denounced as "robber barons" and "lords of industry," equating them with the unproductive, oppressive aristocracy that ruled the feudal ages. Today, we condemn Big Tech, Big Pharma, Big Oil, Big Auto, Big Ag, and any other successful business as greedy and exploitative. To be "Big," i.e., successful, *is* to be bad. According to Rep. Alexandria Ocasio-Cortez: "No one ever makes a billion dollars. You take a billion dollars. . . . You sat on a couch while thousands of people were paid modern-day slave wages."[8]

Tarred as greedy and exploitative, businessmen become convenient scapegoats for every problem or crisis. Who took the blame for the Great Depression? Businessmen. Who took the blame for spiraling healthcare costs? Businessmen. Who took the blame for the 2008 financial crisis? Businessmen. Who took the blame for our recent bout of post-COVID "greedflation"? Businessmen. And despite the reality that each of these crises was caused, not by business, but by anti-capitalist government policy, the scapegoating was used to justify handing even more power to the government.[9] "The greed of Wall Street and corporate America is destroying the very fabric of our nation," claims Sen. Bernie Sanders. "[I]f Wall Street does not end its greed, we will end it for them."[10]

The result of this anti-business rhetoric is an oppressive regulatory state that restricts the freedom of business to build, to innovate, and to profit. Federal regulations take up more than 90,000 pages, with government controls dictating in unimaginable detail how businessmen are permitted to function. Major building projects that took months a century ago now take years to complete (if they can be completed) solely because of regulations like NEPA and

Certificate of Need laws that treat business activity as guilty until proven innocent. And a resurgence in antitrust lawsuits by both Democratic and Republican administrations has threatened our most successful companies precisely because they are successful.[11]

Why We Hate Business

Why is our culture so hostile to business? It's not fundamentally because of any actual wrongs or misdeeds. The reason we evade the achievements of business and vilify businessmen is because we've been taught that their driving motive is dangerous and immoral. "Who on earth," asks conservative luminary Irving Kristol, "wants to live in a society in which all—or even a majority—of one's fellow citizens are fully engaged in the hot pursuit of money, the single-minded pursuit of material self-interest?"[12] You can't trust businessmen for the same reason you can't trust a gangster: he's after money and is willing to do anything and harm anyone in order to get it.

This is utter nonsense. And to see that it's nonsense, ask yourself this question: Why does anyone bother to work? Why does a farmer grow corn or a novelist spend hours a day carefully crafting a story? In short: to make a profit and earn a living.

Human life requires material values, and those values aren't provided ready-made by nature—we have to create them. This is true of our most basic needs for food, clothing, and shelter. But it's true of every value that sustains and enhances our lives. We work in order to eat—and to travel to a friend's wedding, to listen to a soul-nourishing symphony, to spend an afternoon with our children at the zoo. Production is the fuel that powers all of our endeavors, and the proof of successful production is that we have created something more valuable than what we used up, i.e., we have profited.

This is why work itself is so often rewarding. Whether it's a child building a block tower or an architect building a skyscraper or an entrepreneur building a company, there is something deeply fulfilling about exercising the thought and effort necessary to create new values.

The reason that we work, then, is because we value our own lives and our own happiness. To earn a living is an act of self-interest. We seek work that we find rewarding so that we have the material resources to build thriving, joyful lives.

The same is true for businessmen. They seek to earn a living by creating values—and the insignia of value creation in business is monetary profit. To create profits is to build something more valuable. Loss is a signal of destruction. An unproductive employee gets fired. An unproductive businessman goes bankrupt. If you are doing something morally good when you earn a paycheck as a doctor or software developer, then a businessman is doing something morally good when he earns a profit by creating a great business.

Is the problem "too much" profit? There's no such thing. Profits don't come at anyone's expense. They aren't taken from workers or customers. They aren't taken at all. They are earned through countless win/win transactions. An author grows rich because millions of readers value the book more than its cost. A businessman grows rich because thousands or millions or billions of customers value his product more than it cost him to produce it. The greater his profits, the greater the value he has created.

What ensures that a businessman can profit only through creating value rather than through manipulation or exploitation? Freedom. In a truly free society, a businessman cannot force anyone to work for him or to buy from him. Nor can he run to government for favors. His only currency is the opportunities he can offer to others: jobs they want, products they desire, services that enhance their lives.

If a business won't pay me what I think I'm worth, I look for another job (or start my own business). If a company charges me too much or offers me too little, I take my business elsewhere. When people are free, all trade relationships are voluntary, and we only pursue them to the extent they are mutually rewarding.

It is only when people resort to force that someone can profit at another's expense. When an executive defrauds customers he is acting as a thief. When a CEO grows rich on corporate welfare or protectionist tariffs, he is extracting benefits he could not achieve on a free market. But to the extent a society is free, the only path to long-term profitability is virtue: the exercise of rational thought and productive effort necessary to prosper through voluntary trade.

For anyone who values human progress, who recognizes the moral right of each person to grow, thrive, and prosper, who believes that the pursuit of happiness is the individual's noblest quest, then the profit motive represents something good: it is a businessman's desire to earn a living. To build the kind of life he wants to live and the kind of world he wants to live in. To live by his own thought and effort, dealing with others through mutual consent to mutual advantage.

But this is not what we have been taught. The reason we condemn the profit motive is because for more than 2,000 years we have embraced a moral theory that does *not* hold the individual's pursuit of happiness as its goal but selfless service to others. *Altruism*, the moral doctrine that says our duty is to serve something "greater" than ourselves, teaches us that the profit motive *must* be immoral because its aim is not self-sacrifice but self-interest. From the New Testament's condemnation of those who concern themselves with worldly riches—to Marx's condemnation of profit as exploitation—to Martin Luther King, Jr.'s warning that "[t]he profit motive . . . encourages a cutthroat competition and selfish ambition"[13]—to Fed chief Alan Greenspan blaming the "self-interest" of businessmen for a crisis he helped manufacture,[14] we have been indoctrinated with a moral view that teaches us to view businessmen with suspicion at best and hatred at worst.

Altruism distorts our evaluation of business in two basic ways. First, it teaches us that *need*, not achievement, is what entitles a person to values. The economist Thomas Sowell once observed, "I have never understood why it is 'greed' to want to keep the money you have earned but not greed to want to take somebody else's money."[15] The answer, Rand understood, is embedded in the logic of altruism. The morality of altruism allows you to collect sacrifices and gain values—provided you don't *earn* them. If you're a producer, you don't have a right to what you produce. That's greedy. But if you produce nothing? *That* is precisely what gives you a moral right to what others produce. According to altruism, Rand observes, "it is immoral to live by your own effort, but moral to live by the effort of others—it is immoral to consume your own product, but moral to consume the products of others—it is immoral to earn, but moral to mooch—it is the parasites who are the moral justification for the existence of the producers, but the existence of the parasites is an end in itself."[16] To earn a fortune is selfish and immoral. To earn nothing is to be granted a moral blank check on those who create abundance.

Second, altruism teaches us that the only alternative to sacrificing yourself to others is to sacrifice others to yourself. Altruism rejects the possibility of living as a self-supporting trader, who forges mutually rewarding relationships with others. Either you value other people, in which case you must serve and sacrifice for their needs, or you callously ignore other people, in which case you reveal a willingness to trample over their welfare and rights in a brute quest for money, fame, and power. This is why altruists refuse to make a moral distinction between a Steve Jobs and a Bernie Madoff, a Sam Walton and an Al Capone.

But a moral theory that can't distinguish a trader from a thief invalidates itself. A moral theory that casts blame and suspicion on those who create values and legitimizes those who seek to deprive producers of their freedom and their justly earned wealth is deeply unjust. A moral theory that teaches us to condemn the profession that has liberated us from poverty and built a thriving world is suicidal and anti-human.

We need morality. But not the morality of self-sacrifice. "The purpose of morality," said Rand, "is to teach you, not to suffer and die, but to enjoy yourself and live."[17] We need, in short, a morality of self-esteem.[10] One that values each individual's pursuit of happiness.

Why Businessmen Must Stand Up

Businessmen are an oppressed minority. In any conflict with any group—workers, consumers, politicians—they are assumed to be in the wrong. Whatever the problem or crisis, they are assumed to be at fault. When they are subject to special laws scrutinizing, controlling, and penalizing them in a manner that no one else would tolerate, they are expected to shut up and be thankful for how good they have it.

The persecution of businessmen is overlooked because they are not *helpless* victims. Their victimization is not the result of lack of political or financial resources but of *moral* resources. Businessmen are oppressed because they will not stand up for themselves—and they will not stand up for themselves because they accept, or are afraid to challenge, the moral ideal of altruism that dominates our culture.

Altruism paralyzes businessmen. On some level, they know that what they do is good—but they also know that their motive is not the good of others but their own happiness. They know that they are in business because they want to make money doing work they love, not to selflessly serve the needs of others. And so when they encounter arguments that they are achieving "obscene profits" while some people's needs are going unmet, or when they encounter charges that "the public interest" demands reining in their "unchecked greed," they feel mystified, helpless, indignant, and vaguely guilty. Behind closed doors, they might complain about the irrationality of the assault on business. Publicly, they remain silent—or degrade themselves by appeasing and apologizing to their attackers. This isn't merely a practical misstep—it's moral surrender.

This needs to change. Businessmen should stand up for themselves: for the nobility of their profession and their moral right to freedom. Everyone who benefits from the abundance business has created—which means, everyone—has a responsibility to stand up and speak out for business. But if we are to move from business oppression to business liberation, businessmen must not only play a role—they must lead.

Every great movement for justice in American history has required victims of injustice to stand up and say: *I will not accept this any longer.* The American colonists declared their independence from a tyrannical crown. Abolitionists—many of them former slaves—refused to let slavery be accepted as a permanent fact. Women fighting for suffrage stood up and demanded political equality. Civil rights leaders took enormous risks to challenge Jim Crow and demand equal treatment under the law. More recently, the gay pride movement succeeded, not by appealing to pity, but by asserting self-worth: *we will not be treated this way any longer.*[19]

In every case, these movements succeeded when they were animated by the conviction that they were fighting not for special favors or exceptions, but for *justice*—for the recognition that they were moral equals, unjustly persecuted, and deserving of freedom.

Businessmen, too, are the victims of injustice. They are the only group in America routinely denounced not for harming others but for succeeding. They are subject to a regulatory regime built on the premise of *preventive law*—that because they seek profit, they inevitably will do wrong unless subject to surveillance and control. They are presumed guilty before any crime, their freedom preemptively curbed.

And yet, where is the moral outrage? Where are the business leaders declaring: *I am not a servant. I do not apologize for my ability. I do not apologize for earning profits. I am a human being, and I demand to be treated as such*? Until that happens—until businessmen stand up proudly and defiantly—we will continue to live in an anti-business culture that deprives businessmen of the recognition and freedom they deserve. But if they do stand up, history shows what is possible.

Speaking out against injustice can provoke retaliation—from the media, from political activists, from the government. We in no way mean to minimize the risks. But far more dangerous in the long run are the risks of *not* speaking out.

That is why we created the Atlas Circle. The Atlas Circle exists to stand up for business—and to help businessmen stand up for themselves. To provide them with the intellectual ammunition they need to defend the value of their work and to fight for justice and for freedom.

The fight for freedom is never easy, and it never has been. But it is winnable—if those with the most to lose also realize that they have the most to gain by speaking out. The battle for capitalism is, above all, a moral battle. And it can only be won when businessmen rediscover their own moral self-esteem—and demand justice.

OPEN LETTER TO SUNDAR PICHAI AND THE GOOGLE TEAM

January 28, 2025

Dear producers at Google,

For years, you have been a prime target of antitrust persecution. Both private companies and government agencies have sought to strip you of your right to run your business as you see fit, whether it's internet searching, advertising, or an app store. This has culminated, so far, in the Department of Justice asking the court to forcibly take parts of your business away from you.

Your chief legal officer, Kent Walker, has rightly called out the DOJ's "radical interventionist agenda" of breaking up Google. "We wish we were making this up," Walker said, recognizing the devastating nature of DOJ proposals to force Google to sell Chrome or impose a technical committee to micromanage Google's technologies.[1][2] These would destroy the spectacular achievement that Google is.

Walker is right to be alarmed, yet the DOJ's demands are more than legal overreach. It is vital that you, and every other productive American, realize that you are victims of a profound injustice. Like IBM, Microsoft, and many other successful companies before Google, you are being subjected to a witch hunt.

Antitrust enforcers accuse you of exercising "monopoly power," a deliberately vague and undefined notion. The only rational meaning of "monopoly power" is when a government grants to business, say an airline, the exclusive privilege to operate in the country, sealing the business from competition by legally prohibiting other companies from entering the field. Obviously, Google has been granted no such privilege.

To fend off the accusations that you wield some undefined "monopoly power," you laid out a mountain of evidence demonstrating that you have earned and continue to earn your success, even in the face of immediate and constant competitive pressure.[3] You discussed the "emergence of other search competitors," explaining that your market share is not due to the lack of rivals.[4] You argued that even when your ad auction prices are higher than those of competitors, they "yield the best ROI [return on investment]," which your customers willingly pay for. You showcased how you "repeatedly outcompeted [your] rivals . . . on the basis of . . . superior quality and monetization," and your superior "business acumen," like anticipating increased demand in mobile search and investing in it early. And you showed how users go above and beyond to switch back to Google when it is not the default search engine, proving their voluntary commitment to your products.

You hoped that laying out the facts of your competitive business environment and your foresight within it, of which the above is only a small sample, would disarm your attackers. Yet they are undeterred. Do you know why?

All the facts in the world that demonstrate your virtues—your long-range planning, your innovation, your calculated risk-taking, your enormous productivity—will not fend off the antitrust attacks, but *attract* them. In his opinion damning Google as a monopoly, Judge Mehta basically admitted so: "Google is not wrong. It has long been the best search engine.... But these largely undisputed facts are not inconsistent with possessing and exercising monopoly power."[5] Even when you proved that your exclusive agreements to have Google preloaded as the default search engine on smartphones and browsers are a legitimate, voluntary business practice, you were denied equality before the law: "[I]n the hands of a smaller market participant it might be considered harmless, or even honestly industrial," the judge said, referencing a prior court decision. But in the hands of a large, successful firm like yours, it suddenly isn't.

It is not any misconduct that put you on the antitrust "most wanted" list. The court readily acknowledged that your success rests on, as your VP of Regulatory Affairs summarized, "building the best search engine and making smart investment and business decisions," the result of which is that "people don't use Google because they have to—they use it because they want to."[6]

It might be hard to wrap your head around this reality, but antitrust victimizes you precisely *because* of your ability, productivity, and success.

The antitrust system gives its enforcers this power through vaguely written, undefinable, inherently non-objective laws, which Ayn Rand aptly called the "rule of unreason."[7] Charge high prices? Get accused of monopoly pricing. Charge low prices? Get squashed for predatory pricing (like Microsoft, persecuted for giving a browser away for free). Match competitors' prices? "Collusion!" In your case, the issue of exclusive agreements should make clear the arbitrariness of the law: such deals are perfectly legal, unless antitrust enforcers decide that, if Google employs them, they are not.

The most violent criminals know, or at least *can* know, objectively and clearly, when they are violating the law. You, on the other hand, produce life-furthering values on a global scale, but have to live in fear, unable to know if or when antitrust enforcers will descend upon you, declaring your business practices illegal.

Such persecution has no place in America, the only country in history built on the fundamental recognition of the individual's right to live, produce, and trade in freedom, under the rule of law. Americans used their freedom to innovate and build unprecedented wealth. The more some excelled, however, the more some responded not with gratitude but with animosity. Increasingly, as Rand observed, instead of being left free and protected, producers are "at the mercy of the whim, the favor, or the malice of any publicity-seeking politician, any scheming statist, any envious mediocrity who might chance to work his way into a bureaucratic job and who feels a yen to do some trust-busting."[8]

Standard Oil was broken up for succeeding in selling the cheapest oil in the world and thus acquiring more than 90% of the market. Microsoft was dragged through hellish courts for succeeding in building a dominant software ecosystem and products like Office that became industry standards. As countless others who have faced the antitrust inquisition for their achievements, you have become the target for standing at the pinnacle of online search and advertising.

Though antitrust inquisitors might claim to pursue goals like "promoting competition" or "protecting consumers," that can't be their driving motive. If it were, they wouldn't ignore every piece of evidence of your competitors continuing to strategize and devise new products, always ready to step in should you fail to satisfy your customers and partners, whose voluntary choice of your products is the only thing that keeps you at the top. Whether it's to take your wealth, technology, know-how, and serve it on a silver platter to envious competitors, or simply to drag you down just because they can, destroying you is their driving concern.

Whether they admit it or not, the antitrust inquisitors punish the able for exercising their ability, the successful for achieving their success. Next time they announce that they stand for fairness in competition, remember that "fairness" for them means tying your arms behind your back while distributing the fruits of your work to your rivals.

What can you do in response? We are not lawyers and have no legal advice to offer you. But if, in the court of public opinion, you and others in your shoes defend yourselves in *moral* terms, you can help expose the antitrust laws for the evil that they are and help to relegate them, eventually, to the trash bin of history. Let everybody know that the antitrust system is inherently corrupt, that the case against you is profoundly unjust, and that you are proud of your business achievements, which call for moral admiration and celebration, not persecution. For our part, if Ayn Rand has taught us anything, she has taught us to value productive achievements and the individuals whose moral virtues fuel those achievements. The Department of Justice is supposed to represent the people. In persecuting you for your achievements, it does not speak for any of us at the Ayn Rand Institute. It is in the interest of every productive American publicly to proclaim the same. If enough of us do so, we can help end this injustice.

Onkar Ghate, Ph.D., Chief Philosophy Officer and Senior Fellow

Robertas Bakula, Graduate Center Associate

Elan Journo, Vice President of Content and Senior Fellow

Tal Tsfany, President and CEO

A version of this article originally published on January 29, 2025 in Atlas Circle, *a Substack of the Ayn Rand Institute.*

STANDING UP TO DEI ACTIVISM
A Guide for Executives

Don Watkins

Executive Summary

Diversity, Equity, and Inclusion (DEI) was sold as a way to empower your business by rooting out bigotry. Instead, you are under pressure as never before: to mouth slogans you don't agree with, promote causes you don't believe in, to introduce policies and practices that aren't aligned with your company's mission.

In the name of "diversity" you are ordered to hire people based on their group identity, especially on the basis of sex and skin color. In the name of "equity" you are ordered to redistribute power and resources to achieve equal outcomes for "oppressed" groups.

In the name of "inclusion" you are ordered to police speech and behavior that offends "oppressed" groups.

This is no accident. DEI activists are motivated by a radical ideology opposed to business, capitalism, Americanism, and colorblindness. In their view, the world is made up of groups with power oppressing groups without power. Our capitalist system is designed to protect and reward oppressors; the solution is to transform and overthrow the system by redistributing power from oppressors to the oppressed.

That starts in the boardroom. It ends in Washington.

DEI activists aim to use you and your company as tools to achieve their political and social goals. You have a responsibility—to yourself, your shareholders, and the team that you lead—to question those goals, to understand the threat they pose to your business, and to oppose DEI activism in a way that is principled but practical.

This guide for executives explains the theory behind DEI activism, how DEI initiatives harm companies, and the steps businesses can and should take to counter DEI activism. It also includes high-level messaging for companies that can reframe the debate and put DEI activists on the defensive.

Talking Points for Executives

We believe in individual choice and character.

- We believe that individuals are defined by their own character, choices, and actions—not by their group identity.

- Our commitment is to find the individuals who can make the best contribution to our company's mission and pay them accordingly.

We believe in justice.

- We believe in rewarding individuals according to what they earn.

- We reject "equity" or any other goal that rewards or penalizes individuals for reasons other than their productive contributions to our organization's mission.

- We reject as bigotry any call to discriminate against or in favor of individuals on the basis of characteristics such as skin color or sex.

- Our commitment is to identify and remove any barriers to fairness so that all of our team members can thrive.

We believe in capitalism.

- We believe that capitalism is the only system that allows individuals to pursue their own success and happiness by protecting their rights and freedom: the free market unleashes the power of the human mind and the entrepreneurial energy of every worker.

- We proudly support capitalism, which protects the inviolate right of every human being to cooperate with others voluntarily for mutual benefit or to chart their own course.

- We believe that historical injustices like slavery represent the failure to live up to capitalist ideals—they are not grounds for condemning capitalism.

- Our commitment is to champion freedom and use our freedom to create the best company and the best products we can.

The DEI Bait and Switch

Here's the bait: You can strengthen your company by embracing Diversity, Equity, and Inclusion (DEI) initiatives. DEI will allow you to hire the best people and get the best from the people you hire.

Here's the switch: To obey the dictates of DEI, you must weaken your company by policies and practices that order you not to hire the best people and that guarantee you won't get the best from the people you hire.

Who should you select for your Board? The best candidate—unless that candidate has the wrong skin color. Who should you promote to run your marketing department? The best candidate—unless the best candidate is the wrong sex. What policies should you institute and enforce? The policies that will get the best out of your people—unless those policies have been deemed "culturally insensitive" by DEI activists.

But if embracing DEI will hurt the productivity of your company, won't it at least help you avoid controversy and expensive legal battles? It won't. Facebook, for example, has been a pioneer in addressing diversity concerns. It spent hundreds of millions on DEI initiatives, won numerous equality and diversity awards, and garnered a 100% score on the Human Rights Campaign (HRC) 2019 Corporate Equality

Index (CEI).[1] Yet, in 2021, an operations program manager and two job applicants filed a charge of "systemic" racial bias with the Equal Employment Opportunity Commission, alleging that Facebook was showing a "systemic racial bias" against black candidates and employees.[2]

DEI was sold as a way to empower your business. Instead, you are under pressure as never before: to mouth slogans you don't agree with, promote causes you don't believe in, to introduce policies and practices that aren't aligned with your company's mission.

DEI activists aim to use you and your company as tools to achieve their political and social goals. You have a responsibility—to yourself, your shareholders, and the team that you lead—to question those goals, to understand the threat they pose to your business, and to oppose DEI activism in a way that is principled but practical.

Why Executives are Vulnerable to DEI

A 2020 Conference Board global survey of CEOs and other C-suite executives found that the top concern for business leaders is: how to attract and retain top talent.[3] That's unsurprising. Talent is the lifeblood of an organization, and spotting talent, retaining talent, and aligning talent with the goals of the organization are some of the most complex challenges executives face.

Outsiders who have never made a hiring decision will speak about "two equally qualified candidates" differentiated only by race or sex. Executives who have been in the trenches know better.

Who should lead sales at your startup? A former senior VP at a Fortune 500 company? A sales manager who has built and managed large sales teams? A top salesperson without management experience? The former CEO of a recently failed startup who can bring entrepreneurialism to the role? On paper all of these candidates may look "equally qualified." In reality, one may help your company become the next unicorn, while the others may set you back or even put you out of business.

To succeed, business leaders need to make the best decision. And to make the best decision, they need to think deeply about *individuals*—about who has the skills and experience for the position, about who will fit well into your corporate culture, about who will stick around long enough to make an impact on your goals. To place any consideration above who will be the best person for the job is suicidal.

That's why successful executives are always looking for advice about how to improve at spotting talent—and how to identify their talent blindspots. This includes identifying ways that bigotry can be undermining their business goals. To find, attract, and retain the best talent, good executives will be interested in establishing policies and systems that root out bias and discrimination so that talented individuals are hired, promoted, and treated as they deserve. They will be motivated to become more sensitive to ways they and others might unknowingly be undervaluing the contributions of people from different backgrounds or speaking in ways that are insulting or demeaning. They will strive to create a workplace committed to a single ideal: doing great work.

But DEI activists aren't aiming to root out bigotry so that you can profit by hiring the best talent, regardless of sex or skin color. In her book *The Anti-Racist Organization*, HR consultant Shereen Daniels scorns, "Business cases for diversity and inclusion" that "waxed lyrical about the top-line and bottom-line growth that comes with having 'diverse' teams. Even in our oppression, we continued to be exploited by white people for commercial gain."[4] But if helping you become more productive and profitable isn't what DEI activists are after, what is their goal?

DEI in Theory

Executives know that their business lives or dies with talent. The profit motive is a powerful force for encouraging organizations to hire talent regardless of background and to treat employees fairly. Bigotry is not absent from business, but the business case against bigotry is clear-cut: to the extent you root it out, you prosper. To the extent you don't, you lose.

DEI activists appeal to this basic truth about business when selling their agenda, which they define in vague ways designed to obscure their real meaning:

- Diversity: Hiring people of different backgrounds and with different life experiences
- Equity: Ensuring everyone has the same opportunities tailored to their own special needs and circumstances
- Inclusion: Ensuring all team members feel like they belong

DEI advocates intend for executives to interpret this as "Avoid bias, assemble the best team to help you achieve your goals, and treat each member fairly." But that is not what this means—not even close. To see what it actually means, take Ibram Kendi's discussion of equity in his #1 *New York Times* bestseller *How to Be an Antiracist.* According to Kendi, "Racial inequity (or disparity) is when two or more racial groups are not standing on approximately equal footing," as when a higher proportion of black Americans than white Americans are homeless.[5] To rectify unequal outcomes, says Kendi, we cannot treat individuals the same, regardless of skin color. Instead, we must discriminate on the basis of race.

> [I]f racial discrimination is defined as treating, considering, or making a distinction in favor of or against an individual based on that person's race, then racial discrimination is not inherently racist. The defining question is whether the discrimination is creating equity or inequity. If discrimination is creating equity, then it is antiracist. If discrimination is creating inequity, then it is racist.[6]

DEI presents itself as common sense, but in reality, it reflects a radical worldview. This worldview emerged from arcane academic doctrines such as Critical Race Theory, Postmodernism, Marxism, and Kantian Idealism. But behind the complexity lie three key ideas.

(**1**) **Anti-Individualism**: *The group, not the individual, is what counts.*

Individualism is the moral principle that people should be judged as individuals, based on their own choices, actions, and character. Robin DiAngelo, author of the blockbuster *White Fragility*, argues that "the ideology of individualism" is a racist doctrine that promotes the myth that individual merit and hard work are rewarded.[7]

DEI activists, by contrast, see the world in terms of groups: you are little more than your group identity. Kim Wilson, in her book *Diversity, Equity, and Inclusion in the Workplace*, says that "our essential traits" are not our chosen convictions, values, and character but "race, ethnicity, gender, sexuality, and ability status."[8] Our outcomes, in turn, are mainly the product of how society rewards some groups with power and privilege and denies power and privilege to other groups.

(**2**) **Egalitarianism:** *Social justice requires equal outcomes for all groups.*

Anti-individualism tells us what's true about people: they are essentially members of groups and have power and privilege according to their group membership. Egalitarianism tells us what to do about it: sacrifice the powerful and privileged oppressor groups for the sake of oppressed groups.

Egalitarians reject the concept of justice—treating individuals as they deserve. Justice, for example, would demand colorblindness. But DEI activists tell us that colorblindness is not an ideal but an evil. "The ideology of color blindness," writes Daniels, "legitimizes practices that maintain racial inequity."[9]

Instead of justice, DEI activists advocate social justice, which, Mary-Frances Winters writes in her book *Racial Justice at Work*, "entails the fair distribution of wealth, opportunities, and privilege."[10] Fair means equal group outcomes. If 20 percent of the people in your community are black, for example, 20 percent of your company should be black. And it's not just the overall makeup of your company that matters: 20 percent of your board should be black, 20 percent of your managers, 20 percent of your computer programmers. Anything less is proof of social injustice, calling for "new, radical remedies that disrupt these stubborn patterns of disproportionate outcomes."[11]

(3) Anticapitalism: *Because capitalism is the system of individualism, it allows powerful groups to oppress less powerful groups.*

DEI is not primarily a management doctrine but a political one, which is why many of its efforts are not aimed at reforming companies but at pressuring companies to reform society.

What is DEI's vision of society? Racism and other forms of bigotry, they say, are built into the capitalist system and Western civilization. "Capitalism," writes Kendi, "in producing racial injustices and inequities between race-classes, is essentially racist."[12] As a result, "Antiracist policies cannot eliminate class racism without anticapitalist policies."[13]

Indeed, racism is at the root of Western culture as such: "the founding principles upon which Western society is built purposefully created the racist ideology we live by," writes Daniels.[14]

This is the DEI ideology: DEI activists see a world made up of groups with power oppressing groups without power. Our capitalist system is designed to protect and reward oppressors; the solution is to transform and overthrow the system by redistributing power from oppressors to the oppressed. That starts in the boardroom. It ends in Washington.

We can now go beyond the vague definitions of Diversity, Equity, and Inclusion found in HR manuals to their full meanings.

Diversity

- Vague meaning: Hiring people of different backgrounds and with different life experiences

- Full meaning: Hiring people based on their group identity, especially on the basis of sex and skin color

Equity

- Vague meaning: Ensuring everyone has the same opportunities tailored to their own special needs and circumstances
- Full meaning: Redistributing power and resources to achieve equal outcomes for "oppressed" groups

Inclusion

- Vague meaning: Ensuring all team members feel like they belong
- Full meaning: Policing speech and behavior that offends "oppressed" groups

DEI in Practice

According to DEI activists, every organization is bigoted. We know this without having to point to unfair treatment. We know this because no organization does or can perfectly reflect the race/sex/gender identity/sexual identity/class/disability status mix of its community—and because no organization can avoid offending some "oppressed" group by violating some inclusivity rule that sprang into existence within the last five years (or five minutes). In her DEI workshops, Robin DiAngelo puts it bluntly: "The question is not 'did racism take place'? but rather 'how did racism manifest in that situation?'"[15]

You are guilty until proven innocent—and you cannot prove your innocence.

The harm is made worse by the implication that your employees are either bigots who need you to make them into good people or victims who need you to coddle them. This patronizing implication will be reinforced to a greater or lesser degree depending on the specific training you authorize. Often these training sessions consist of indoctrination into the ideas of the most radical DEI activists. At AT&T, for example, employees were invited to

> "do one action to further your understanding of power, privilege, supremacy, oppression, and equity" every day for 21 days. These actions include reading, watching, or listening to material on antiracism, gender issues, and/or social justice from an ideologically uniform list that features Ibram X. Kendi, Robin DiAngelo, Ta-Nehisi Coates, and Nikole Hannah-Jones. No alternative or critical point of view is listed.[16]

A mandatory DEI training program offered to employees of the City of Seattle taught

> that white male individuals ... "are bolstered by racism," that they "internalize it," and that "individuals, institutions, and communities are often unconsciously and habitually rewarded for supporting white privilege and power." [Employees] were taught that "racism is in white people's DNA" and that many seemingly normal office behaviors—including a "focus on timeline" and an "emphasis on being polite"—were actually "manifestations of white supremacy culture."

Is it any surprise that *The Washington Post* can point to a "range of past social science studies that have shown that efforts to reduce prejudice can backfire—actually increasing bias or leading to more hostility rather than less"?[17]

Ask yourself: are you prepared to inject racial discrimination into your company? Are you prepared to deny promotions to talented individuals because of their skin color? Are you prepared to poison your corporate culture with training designed to stir up grievances and inculcate guilt? And if not, are you prepared to oppose it?

DEI Tactics and How to Oppose Them

Executives struggle to deal with DEI activism because DEI activists understand something they don't: the power of moral logic. In her essay "The Anatomy of Compromise," philosopher Ayn Rand describes three key principles of moral logic:

1. In any *conflict* between two men (or two groups) who hold the same basic principles, it is the more consistent one who wins.

2. In any *collaboration* between two men (or two groups) who hold *different* basic principles, it is the more evil or irrational one who wins.

3. When opposite basic principles are clearly and openly defined, it works to the advantage of the rational side; when they are *not* clearly defined but are hidden or evaded, it works to the advantage of the irrational side.[18]

DEI activists know that if they can get a company to agree to the principles of DEI, then they will hold the moral high ground in any conflict. And so their demands always start small and then escalate. Here is the common pattern:

1. Ask for small concessions, such as a generic commitment to DEI, in your annual report.
2. Argue that your company is failing to live up to its commitments.
3. Deploy internal, public, financial, regulatory, and legal pressure to demand increasingly intrusive and radical actions and policies.

For example, in 2023, Bloomberg Law cataloged how dozens of lawsuits have been filed against companies such as Delta and Wells Fargo, charging that they are failing to live up to their DEI commitments.

> Many companies were quick to make statements and incorporate new policies to address racial, ethnic, and gender inequality among their employee ranks after George Floyd's murder in 2020. Those new policies have been cited in numerous employee and investor suits, with more expected if companies fail to fully integrate DEI pledges into their workforce and board level operations, labor attorneys and DEI consultants said.[19]

Executives typically think they can appease activists with low-cost actions, such as vague assurances that their company is committed to diversity, equity, and inclusion. But appeasement doesn't work. Instead, it handicaps your ability to level a principled opposition to DEI pressure. Per Rand's first rule, in a contest between two parties who declare that DEI is good, the more consistent, more radical side will hold the moral high ground while the less consistent side will come across as groveling and insincere.

Executives face a choice. They can either commit to going all the way and embracing DEI activism as a central feature of their company—or they can oppose it on principle.

What they can't do is find some stable middle ground. Any "middle ground" simply means being forced into a defensive posture where executives must explain why they aren't doing more, why they aren't achieving the results they've committed to, why they aren't speaking up about the latest cultural controversy, why they aren't doing everything that DEI activists demand of them.

The Positive Alternative You'll Need

To oppose DEI on principle requires that you be principled—that you have a positive set of values governing your decisions. A company that merely says no to DEI opens itself up to charges of bigotry—but a company that says no to DEI because the DEI ideology is at odds with its values can own the moral high ground and inoculate itself from further attacks.

- Contrast "We don't do DEI" with "We aim to find the best individuals for our organization and so oppose demands that we judge people on the basis of skin color."

- Contrast "We believe in diversity, equity, and inclusion" with "We believe in treating individuals as individuals, focusing on a person's choices, character, competence and ability to help further our organization's mission."

- Contrast "We stand with #BlackLivesMatter" with "We stand for American ideals like individual rights, political freedom, legal equality, and capitalism, which make our business possible—and we demand that America live up to those ideals so every American can flourish."

When executives explain their choices in moral terms and appeal to their own genuinely held values, they reverse the pattern that empowers DEI activists. As Rand's third rule notes, "When opposite basic principles are clearly and openly defined, it works to the advantage of the rational side." A business that rejects DEI on principle faces more pressure at the start—it is harder to say "we oppose the DEI ideology" than it is to cut and paste a vague endorsement of DEI in its annual report. But this changes the dynamics of the debate thereafter.

Executives will not be vulnerable to DEI shaming because they have not endorsed the standards DEI activists use to shame them. On the contrary, executives can turn the tables and put DEI activists on the defensive by showing that the activists oppose the company's values—values that even today have the power to garner widespread support. *Most people do not support the unsanitized DEI ideology.*

Business has been vulnerable to DEI attacks, not because it has opposed them, but because it has tried to comply with them partway. If you can explain in clear, common-sense terms that you reject the radical DEI ideology because you value individual ability and character, you may not avoid controversy—no business today can avoid controversy—but you will own the moral high ground.

Instead of feeling defensive, instead of having to mouth slogans you don't really believe and sign off on programs you don't really support, you can speak your mind—and win public support.

The Words You'll Need

Just as companies must formulate winning messages for new product campaigns, they need to formulate winning messages for intellectual campaigns. Below are sample messages that will allow you to use moral logic in your own favor.

We believe in individual choice and character.

- We believe that individuals are defined by their own character, choices, and actions—not by their group identity.
- Our commitment is to find the individuals who can make the best contribution to our company's mission and pay them accordingly.

We believe in justice.

- We believe in rewarding individuals according to what they earn.
- We reject "equity" or any other goal that rewards or penalizes individuals for reasons other than their productive contributions to our organization's mission.
- We reject as bigotry any call to discriminate against or in favor of individuals on the basis of characteristics such as skin color or sex.
- Our commitment is to identify and remove any barriers to fairness so that all of our team members can thrive.

We believe in capitalism.

- We believe that capitalism is the only system that allows individuals to pursue their own success and happiness by protecting their rights and freedom: the free market unleashes the power of the human mind and the entrepreneurial energy of every worker.

- We proudly support capitalism, which protects the inviolate right of every human being to cooperate with others voluntarily for mutual benefit or to chart their own course.

- We believe that historical injustices like slavery represent the failure to live up to capitalist ideals—they are not grounds for condemning capitalism.

- Our commitment is to champion freedom and use our freedom to create the best company and the best products we can.

The Tactics You'll Need

Different organizations operate in different contexts. Executives of businesses in the public eye or in heavily regulated industries have to approach the DEI challenge differently from other executives. Insofar as executives are operating at the point of a gun, they are constrained in their ability to oppose DEI.

What we advocate is not that executives become martyrs or that they expose their company to unnecessary legal or political risk. But we believe there is more scope for a company that has defined a positive set of values to take a principled stance against DEI than generally believed.

Here are five tactics every executive can use to stand up to DEI activists:

1. *Speak out when you can speak out.* The fact that an executive may be partially constrained in their ability to oppose DEI activism does not justify across-the-board silence and certainly not disingenuous support for DEI. If a company is forced to comply with a DEI initiative, it can communicate that it is doing so in compliance with the law—not because the initiative reflects its own convictions. And if an executive cannot openly oppose DEI while at the helm of a company, they can and should oppose it once they leave the company, including by making clear to the public the kind of pressure tactics CEOs face behind the scenes.

2. *Minimize the damage.* Insofar as an organization has to comply with DEI demands, there are still better and worse ways to comply. For example, organizations may have to offer DEI training, but there are an increasing number of diversity training organizations that reject the DEI ideology.[20] Similarly, executives can ensure that they

do not hire DEI activists to oversee their DEI efforts.

3. *Stop funding the universities and other sources of DEI activism.* The DEI ideology was created in and continues to be powered by the universities.[21] More generally, universities are the main source of ideas hostile toward individualism, opportunity, capitalism, and America.[22] Executives should refuse to provide the financial support that fuels their attackers.

4. *Start or increase funding for individuals and organizations who promote your actual ideals.* However constrained executives are in their own ability to speak out, they have the power to promote their values by funding those who can speak out.

5. *Don't support anti-freedom policies designed to suppress DEI.* Anti-freedom policies achieve nothing positive. DEI activists will simply change their language or tactics. For example, faced with a political backlash against DEI in Tennessee, the UT system's Division of Diversity and Engagement simply rebranded itself the Division of Access and Engagement.[23] Worse, by conceding that the government should have the power to control and suppress ideas, DEI opponents are handing the government a tool that *can and will be used against them.* If the government can suppress the DEI ideology, it can suppress criticism of DEI. If the government can suppress anti-

capitalist speech, it can suppress pro-capitalist speech. DEI opponents should be principled defenders of freedom and free speech.

Next Steps

DEI activists have succeeded by using the power of moral logic against business. But the activists are vulnerable. Their strategy only works to the extent they can mask their true goals and to the extent you fail to articulate a superior alternative.

The fact is that there is a silent majority who do not believe in judging people by their skin color or other physical characteristics, who do not believe that individualism is evil, and who do not believe that America and Western civilization are essentially racist and immoral.

Business leaders have traditionally ignored the realm of ideas and avoided taking intellectual stands that seem risky and controversial. If it was ever possible to avoid taking intellectual stands, it no longer is. DEI activists have insisted that individualism, the opposite of racism, is racism.

Given the reality that you must take a stand, you should proactively take a stand on your own terms and in the name of your own values.

You owe it to yourself and to the people you lead.

A version of this article origionally published on January 27, 2025 in Atlas Circle, *a Substack of the Ayn Rand Institute.*

ATLAS SHRUGGED
America's Second Declaration of Independence

Onkar Ghate

AYN RAND'S NOVEL *Atlas Shrugged* is selling far more today, over 500,000 copies in 2009, than in its first year of sales after publication in 1957. In the midst of the current massive growth in the government's power over the economy—financial bailouts, "emergency powers" exerted over the banking system, trillions in spending, soaring deficits, more state-run health care added to existing programs like Social Security and Medicare that already have trillions of dollars in unfunded liabilities—in the midst of all this, Americans are right to turn to Rand's epic novel.

For far more than just a story containing an eerily similar situation (the novel depicts the economic breakdown of the United States), *Atlas Shrugged* offers us an explanation for why, decade after decade, the government's power continues to expand and, even more important, a way out. It presents the ideas we must implement to reverse course. Indeed, in my estimation, *Atlas Shrugged* is nothing short of America's second Declaration of Independence.

To understand this radical claim, we need to begin by rewinding some 230 years, to the birth of the nation, to consider both what the American Revolution accomplished and what it failed to accomplish. It is easy to forget how new an idea America is. The Founding Fathers invented a new type of government. All previous forms of government had, to some degree or other, placed power in the hands of the state at the expense of the individual.

Theocracy placed power in the hands of priests and popes, who, as spokesmen for the supernatural, were to be obeyed without question. Monarchy placed power in the hands of a king or queen, whose subjects lived and died by the ruler's edicts. Aristocracy placed power in the hands of a hereditary elite, who trampled on the members of the lower classes. Democracy placed power in the hands of the majority, who could do what they wished to any minority.

In all these systems, recalcitrant individuals were dealt with in the same way. They were greeted with the instruments of physical compulsion: with imprisonment, torture, and death.

The priests placed Galileo under house arrest and burned Bruno at the stake. The king beheaded Thomas More. The aristocrats butchered individual peasants en masse. The Athenian democracy forced Socrates to drink hemlock.

To all such outrages, the Founding Fathers said: No more.

They devised a system that placed power into the hands of the *individual* at the expense of the state. The individual, they declared, possesses the inalienable rights to life, liberty, property, and the pursuit of happiness. The government does not stand above the individual, as his master, but *below* him, as his servant.

"To secure these rights," Jefferson wrote in the Declaration of Independence, "governments are instituted among men, deriving their just powers from the consent of the governed." If a government trespasses on the rights of the individual, "it is the right of the people to alter or to abolish it, and to institute new government."

In the Declaration, the Founding Fathers were of course declaring political independence from Britain. More deeply, however, they were declaring independence from priests and from kings, from aristocrats and from the will of the majority.

They were creating a sanctuary for *individuals* with unbowed minds—for the Galileos and Socrateses of the world, who were henceforth to meet with a different fate.

What motivated the Founding Fathers to take the enormously dangerous action of creating a new country? Why did they risk their lives, their fortunes, and their sacred honor?

The key to understanding their motivation is that they were this-worldly, fact-based idealists.

As students of the Enlightenment, of Europe's Age of Reason, the Founding Fathers believed in the perfectibility of man. If man unfailingly uses his rational mind, and if he carefully studies and formulates the methods by which in fact human values and prosperity are achieved, then perfection, they held, here on earth, is within man's grasp.

This, precisely, is what the Founding Fathers did with regard to the subject of government. They painstakingly studied the forms and history of governments, in order to define a perfect method of governance. The result was the Constitution of the United States, with its innovative set of checks and balances, designed to prevent any emergence of absolute power.

To most British subjects, British rule was good (which, comparatively speaking, it was) and good enough. But to the Founding Fathers, good was not good enough. As idealists, they sought perfection. When they saw the possibility for action, therefore, they rebelled—when few other men would have done so.

To burn with this type of idealism requires a profound self-esteem. It requires a spirit that wants to see perfection made real, for itself and in its own life. Genuine self-esteem—not the "we're all okay" variety—is an earned esteem of your own soul. It is the conviction that you are deserving of success and happiness, because you are continuously working to achieve these.

If you wonder about the imposing stature of the Founding Fathers, of men like Washington, Franklin, and Jefferson, this is the key. They were men of genuine self-esteem; men who took the perfection of their own lives, mind, character, and happiness with the utmost seriousness. They were abstract thinkers and also doers: men of wide and constantly expanding erudition, who were also lawyers, farmers, printers, business owners, architects, and inventors.

This kind of individual will jealously guard his freedom—his freedom to follow his own judgment, to make his own choices, and to enjoy the values and wealth he creates. To such an individual, the issue of his own perfectibility is a daily reality, which he will allow no one to usurp. To such an individual, the idea that he is a sinful or irrational or wretched creature, desperately in need of a superior to tell him what to do, has no reality. This kind of an individual will allow no king or government to dictate his convictions or dispose of his fortune and life—not for any reason or to any degree.

For the Founding Fathers, the motto "live free or die" had real meaning. Without freedom, they would be dead—their mode of existence would be dead—their unrelenting, unbowed pursuit of their own perfection would be dead. And so they fought. The Declaration of Independence was a declaration of self-esteem. It was signed by men proud to fight for their *full* freedom.

But their achievement is eroding.

The Founding Fathers would be shocked by the power that is now concentrated in the hands of the American government at the expense of the individual.

Can you imagine Thomas Jefferson submitting to building inspectors, who would decide if Monticello is up to government code? Pleading with FDA officials to be allowed to take an experimental drug that, according to his own scientific judgment, would be beneficial for him to take? Allowing Social Security administrators to dictate how much he has to save for retirement and where he can invest it? Patiently watching the tax collector take his money and pour it down the aid drains of the Middle East and Africa? Prostrating himself before the FCC, which would determine whether or not his broadcast content is obscene? Can you imagine Thomas Jefferson seeking the government's permission to eat irradiated spinach, screw in an incandescent light bulb, or buy a trans-fatty French fry? Would he allow the government to thus dictate to him what he ought and ought not to do? The answer is obvious.

Today, however, Americans do not have the self-esteem to protest these usurpations of their judgment, their choice, their freedom.

America's declaration of self-esteem has *not* taken full root.

Why not?

Although the core of self-esteem is an earned confidence in one's power to think and to produce—which

Americans have earned in abundance—full self-esteem requires that one *self-consciously* value one's self. Full self-esteem requires that one know in explicit, moral terms that one is good—and why.

This moral conviction neither the Declaration of Independence nor any other writing of the Founding Fathers provides Americans.

Consider why this is so. The European Enlightenment had promised to put morality on a rational, mathematically precise foundation, but it could never deliver on its promise. And far too many of its intellectual leaders assumed that the content of morality would be essentially Christian morality, stripped of its mystical trappings, and, somehow, defended by rational argument. The Founding Fathers agreed with the European intellectuals.

Jefferson, for instance, made his own compilation of Jesus' teachings. Jefferson's compilation, which omits the miraculous from the New Testament, includes the Sermon on the Mount. Indeed, Jefferson in a letter refers to Jesus as "the sublime preacher of the sermon on the mount."

But ask yourself this: Does the Sermon on the Mount not indict Jefferson and the other Founding Fathers?

When the British struck America's right cheek, did Jefferson in the Declaration tell America to turn to offer them the left? Did Jefferson love his enemy—or did he go to war with him? Did Jefferson, who had a gallery of worthies in his home, portraits of men like Isaac Newton and John Locke, think that the blessed are the poor in spirit—or that the only people worthy of admiration are those who choose to make something of their spirit? Did Jefferson and the other Founding Fathers think that the meek shall inherit the earth—or that, in Locke's words, the rational and the industrious shall? Did Jefferson give up riches—or did he seek them?

On every essential, the Founding Fathers did the opposite of what the Sermon commands.

And that's because the Sermon on the Mount *is a declaration of war on man's self-esteem.*

Anyone who has achieved anything and taken pride and joy in his accomplishments, is condemned by Jesus. "Woe unto you that are rich! for ye have received your consolation. Woe unto you that are full! for ye shall hunger. Woe unto you that laugh now! for ye shall mourn and weep."

Who then has a right to feel good about themselves, according to the Sermon? The meek and the poor in spirit—which means: those who have no cause to esteem themselves.

This is the key to understanding the direction of America's political history.

The Founding Fathers created a new form of government and thereby opened up a continent to their kind of individuals—individuals of self-esteem, individuals who were ready to drop their old, backward cultures and work for a better future, individuals who valued themselves so highly that they sought the best for themselves and in themselves by coming to America.

But the Founding Fathers left these individuals unable fully to understand or appreciate their own greatness, open to every form of abuse, and vulnerable to every sort of moral denunciation from a moral code that had dominated the Old World for centuries.

And the denunciations soon came. The new country had exploded with breathtaking feats of productivity. Most responsible for this prosperity were individuals who had never had a chance to exist before: capitalists and industrialists. Oil, steel, railroads, new financial instruments—these and other innovations the Rockefellers, the Carnegies, the Vanderbilts, and the J. P. Morgans brought into the New

World and taught men how to value. For this, they were denounced as robber barons.

In essence, it was Jesus' voice rising against them: "Woe unto you that are rich! For ye shall suffer; woe unto you that build railroads and oil derricks! For ye shall mourn and weep."

But *more* than just moral denunciations came. If America was to be the land of the *ideal*, as the Founding Fathers had promised, and if the ideal is in fact that the meek and poor in spirit shall inherit the earth, then America's government needed *drastic* overhaul.

All the new governmental powers, the alphabet soup of regulatory agencies that Jefferson would have rebelled against, were *justified* by attacking the men of self-esteem in the name of the meek and the poor in spirit.

What is the *moral* justification, for instance, for the FDA's existence? Rich, greedy drug companies—i.e., those who discover and manufacture life-saving pharmaceuticals—will exploit and experiment on hapless patients, so the government must oversee the companies' every move. Besides, how can the meek be served, unless the government, through its approvals and rejections, favors the kinds of drugs the meek need? And how can the poor in spirit achieve blessedness, if in their mindlessness they ingest a pill that they could have known might kill them? So to protect the blessed from their own ignorance or irrationality, we need wise government officials to approve drugs and dictate to everyone what pills he may and may not swallow.

Or what is the *moral* justification for the creation of Social Security? To quote from the Administration's website, in an article about the history of social security, it is "the government's duty to provide for the welfare of the poor." If a person is too meek to provide for his own old age, then those who are richer should be forced to provide for his retirement. If a person is too ignorant or irresponsible to save for his own retirement—if he is that poor in spirit—then the government must step in and, in his name, strip everyone of control over his retirement plans.

Or what was the *moral* justification for the income tax, ratified in 1913? "Soak the rich."

Now to *all* of this—to whatever form the sacrifice of men of achievement and self-esteem to men without achievement and self-esteem takes—Ayn Rand in *Atlas Shrugged* says: No more.

In one of the world's great acts of independence, Rand declares, in effect, that the essence of the

Sermon on the Mount, along with everything it presupposes and everything it implies, is evil.

The idea that the good consists in achieving the good of others—of your neighbors, of your country, or even of your enemies—of anyone or anything, real or imagined, that is *not* you—the idea that you must sacrifice your personal values without even an expectation of return—the idea that nobility means being selfless, and wickedness means being concerned with self—the idea that morality is synonymous with altruism, and immorality synonymous with egoism—all of this is challenged in *Atlas Shrugged*.

Of this whole approach to good and evil, Rand asks questions no one dared to ask.

What, she asks in *Atlas Shrugged*, *is* the good according to this morality? Supposedly, it's that you achieve the good of others. But what then is their good? Presumably, that they in turn achieve the good of still other people. But then we are again faced with the same unanswered question: what is the good of these other people?

To the question "What is the good?" this approach to morality actually provides you with no answer. It gives you only a chain of arrows, leading to nowhere; a string of zeroes, adding up to nothing. The code upholds no ultimate value or positive ideal. It is unconcerned with the main task of the science of ethics: namely, of *defining* the good that you must achieve and live up to.

So what does this do to people in actual practice? It means that it is *impossible* to know whether you have ever achieved the good—or failed in the attempt.

Consider first what this does to a man of self-esteem. To anyone striving to be *good*, this code declares that you have never done enough. No matter how much you've sacrificed, you can never achieve your own moral perfection. You can never reach the ideal.

Have you ever wondered why the demands for sacrifice just continue to grow and grow? The income tax, for instance, started off as something that of course would apply only to the very rich and that of course would be capped at 7% of income. But then it grew to 15%, 20% and 25% of income, and included in its clutches more and more productive citizens. Can we, as productive individuals, at any stage protest that we've sacrificed enough, that we've already achieved the good of others? Don't be so naïve—we're answered—who said the good was achievable?

Or why is it that decade after decade, as the United States pours money into Asia, Africa and the Middle East, still more handouts are demanded from us? Can we ever protest that we've sacrificed enough, that we've achieved the good of others? Again the same answer: Surely you're not so naïve as to think the good is achievable?

The result, therefore, to any rational person striving to be good, is a state of moral anxiety, self-doubt, and guilt. No matter how much he has sacrificed, the thought haunts him that to be good he should have sacrificed still more. Many decent people therefore stop striving to be one hundred percent moral—"Not everyone can be a saint," they conclude—and they thereby *abandon the quest for self-esteem.*

Now what of the scoundrels who are actually unconcerned with achieving happiness and moral perfection within their own souls? No matter the nature of their concrete actions or how dreadful the outcomes of those actions so far, so long as their motive is not self-interest, anything is permitted to them. Whatever they do, they retain the halo of morality.

Have you ever wondered why, when the so-called humanitarians at the U.N. produce debacle after debacle and corruption after corruption, their power and prestige only increase? Have you ever wondered why, when government program after government program leads to disaster—when Social Security jeopardizes your financial future, public education turns out barely literate children, and Medicare causes skyrocketing costs—the scope and funding of these programs only increase? Have you ever wondered why, as individuals were murdered in the thousands and tens of thousands in Communist Russia and China, many onlookers in the East and West alike said: Give them more time, they may eventually achieve the good of others?

Atlas Shrugged gives us the answer. *Nothing* can count as failure to achieve the good of others, because nothing counts as *success*.

> 'The good of others' is a magic formula that transforms anything into gold, a formula to be recited as a guarantee of moral glory and as a fumigator for any action, even the slaughter of a continent. . . . You need no proof, no reasons, no success . . .—all you need to know is that your motive was the good of others, *not* your own. Your only definition of the good is a negation: the good is the 'non-good for me.' (*Atlas Shrugged*)

What we have here is a *negative* morality. This code is unable to specify the nature of the good. But it does define, in precise detail, the nature of *evil*. To be concerned with advancing your own interests, is evil; to escape evil, therefore, you must *sacrifice* your values.

The only concrete advice the code offers you is: sacrifice, sacrifice, and then sacrifice some more. This is the real focus of the code and why Rand names it *the morality of sacrifice*.

Sacrifice your money to strangers who have not earned it, proclaims the Sermon on the Mount, and sacrifice your love to enemies who hate you. Sacrifice the values of both matter and spirit. Sacrifice, sacrifice, sacrifice.

But does this morality of sacrifice not contain some enormous, hidden double standard?

As Rand asks in *Atlas Shrugged*:

> Why is it moral to serve the happiness of others, but not your own? . . . Why is it immoral to produce a value and keep it, but moral to give it away? And if it is not moral for you to keep a value, why is it moral for others to accept it? If you are selfless and virtuous when you give it, are they not selfish and vicious when they take it? Does virtue consist of serving vice? Is the . . . purpose of those who are

good, self-immolation for the sake of those who are evil?

Now what, in effect, is the Sermon on the Mount's answer to these questions?

> The ... monstrous answer is: No, the takers are not evil, provided they did not earn the value you gave them. It is not immoral for them to accept it, provided they are unable to produce it, unable to deserve it, unable to give you any value in return. (*Atlas Shrugged*)

Why, for instance, do drug companies *not* have the right to sell their inventions to anyone and everyone eager to buy them? Because the companies invented the drugs. Why do we, the public, through the FDA, have the right to dictate what drugs these companies can and cannot sell, how they must research, test, manufacture, and label them, what uses they can and cannot be prescribed for, and who can purchase them? What gives us this incredible power? The fact that we didn't invent the drugs.

Or why does an employee not have the right to keep and invest all his income as he judges best for his old-age? Because he earned the money. Why do we, the public, through the Social Security Administration, have the right to take part of his income and dole it out to whomever we think needs it? Precisely because we, and the recipients, didn't earn the money.

> Such is the secret core of your creed, the other half of your double standard: it is immoral to live by your own effort, but moral to live by the effort of others—it is immoral to consume your own product, but moral to consume the products of others . . .—it is the parasites who are the moral justification for the existence of the producers, but the existence of the parasites is an end in itself. (*Atlas Shrugged*)

If you want just one example to fix in your mind the gruesome essence of the morality of sacrifice, and what it does to self-esteem, consider America's response to 9/11.

When the Twin Towers were attacked and thousands of individuals killed, many people in the Middle East danced in the streets. But others there, although sympathetic to the revelers, sought to hide the revelry from view. They worried that the attacks had gone too far this time, and that Americans would refuse to suffer such an outrage. They worried that our self-esteem was not completely extinguished, and that their gloating would revive it. They worried about our indignation and our wrath.

And in the immediate aftermath there were some signs of these on the part of Americans. There was anger and desire for revenge. People wanted the President to do something. Responding to the country's mood, the Bush Administration promised a campaign of shock and awe, and the extraction of "Infinite Justice."

But then—there is little doubt—Bush asked himself: "What would Jesus do?" Tragically, it was a question to which Bush knew the answer.

Even as we pursued some of the killers, a more fundamental injunction emerged: we had to love our enemy. Operation Infinite Justice was renamed so as not to offend the Islamic world. Gone was the extraction of justice, replaced by the goal of bringing democracy to the Middle East, so that its inhabitants could elect whomever they wished, killers like Hamas emphatically *not* excluded. A campaign of shock and awe did still materialize—but not in the way originally meant.

Imagine the utter shock of the Islamic warriors and their numerous supporters, when they realized that it was not U.S. bombs dropping on their heads, but packets of lentils, barley stew, biscuits, peanut butter, and strawberry jam, along with the message: "This is a food gift from the people of the United States of America." Imagine the awe they must have felt at their own power.

They had attacked the Pentagon and toppled the Twin Towers, and this had brought them not what it brought the Japanese after Pearl Harbor, namely U.S. soldiers bent on their complete destruction or unconditional surrender, but U.S. soldiers bent on rebuilding their hospitals and mosques and bringing them the vote—the young American soldiers all the while dying in the attempt.

We are proving to these people that the meek shall inherit the earth and that blessed indeed are the poor in spirit. As they regroup in Afghanistan, Pakistan, Iran, and elsewhere, the confidence and power these killers and their numerous supporters feel is real: it is granted to them by the morality of sacrifice.

The Sermon on the Mount and all its variations through the centuries—*Atlas Shrugged* reveals—is a morality *of* evil and *for* evil.

But it has a fatal flaw. It requires that its victims accept it.

> I saw that the enemy was an inverted morality—and that my sanction was its

only power. . . . I saw that there comes a point, in the defeat of any man of virtue, when his own consent is needed for evil to win. . . . I saw that I could put an end to your outrages by pronouncing a single word in my mind. I pronounced it. The word was 'No.' (*Atlas Shrugged*)

This is the beginning of Ayn Rand's declaration of *moral* independence.

To win your moral independence, she declares, you must first say "No" to the corrupt ideal of sacrifice. You must reject as unspeakably evil any morality that demands sacrifices, whether the sacrifice of your values to the misfortune or irrationality of others, or the sacrifice of their values to your misfortune or irrationality.

Whether it be a relative demanding an attention he has not earned, or the latest health-care scheme from Washington promising to give us something for nothing by soaking the rich, we must say "No." The moment the good requires victims—it ceases to be good.

To win your moral independence, you must uphold every individual's moral right to exist—beginning with your own. You have the right to exist, a moral right to your own life and to trying to achieve happiness within its days and years.

No one has a moral right to demand that you gain *his* permission to exist by slavishly ministering to his needs and protecting him from his own shortcomings. No one has a claim on your life. The moment someone waves his pain or need or failures or misfortune around, proclaiming that *these* entitle him to your values, he removes himself from any moral consideration.

The Founding Fathers grasped, politically, that no one gains a right to your life by virtue of his real or alleged *superiority*. Neither priest nor king nor aristocrat nor the majority gains a right to your life by virtue of superior social position, mystic visions, ancestors, wealth, or numbers.

What must now be grasped, morally, is that no one gains a claim to your life by virtue of his real or alleged *inferiority*. No one gains a moral claim to your life by virtue of his inferior wealth, power, happiness, intelligence, health, ability, knowledge, or judgment.

What this means is that your moral stature is not at the mercy of whether someone else has failed, or perhaps could not even be bothered, to provide for his own health care or retirement.

Politically, the Declaration of Independence taught us to reject the notion of undeserved serfdom. Morally, *Atlas Shrugged* teaches us to reject the notion of *unearned guilt*.

In place of unearned guilt, one should embrace the nature of one's existence as an individual human being—a being that must seek and create values in order to remain vibrantly alive.

This is the precondition of self-esteem: to seek in all things the best for one's self.

To embrace life is to recognize that the whole act of valuing arises in the context of one's own life and the need to make it go well. From a child choosing a toy to a teenager choosing a friend to an adult choosing a career or a lover or a form of government—the need to do so arises from the same question: What will advance my life?

The precondition of self-esteem is to refuse, as the Founding Fathers refused, to settle for anything less than the ideal in one's life.

And to this quest for the ideal, the science of morality, properly conceived, is an indispensable aid. Its task is to teach you fully *what* to value and *how* to value. Its task is to teach you how to attain life and happiness.

Atlas Shrugged accordingly offers a new conception of the moral ideal—a new conception of the sacred and the exalted, far different from that of the Sermon on the Mount. Fundamental to its new moral code are the actual requirements of life and happiness. Central to its new ideal, therefore, are the virtues of *thought*, *production*, and *trade*.

Atlas Shrugged is a hymn to man's mind. Every value that man has achieved had to first be discovered by some individual mind or minds. From picking fruits to hunting with spears to planting crops in order to harvest them months later—from the invention of theater, as a source of enjoyment and emotional fuel, to the discovery of perspective in painting to the creation of music—from the identification of the laws of motion to the formulation of the laws of logic—from the discovery of germs and antibiotics to the invention of the transistor and the computer—for each of these steps, some mind had to figure it out. This is the source of human life and happiness. To worship life, therefore, means to worship man's intelligence.

And if it is your *own* life that you seek, then the development of your intelligence becomes the most fundamental of goals. To learn to think, to make connections, and to see farther than you have so far seen—to learn to think carefully, systematically, logically, and objectively—to learn to see the full implications of your ideas—all this becomes the most important of tasks.

The scope of your knowledge and the power of your thinking will dictate the success or failure of all your value pursuits, from earning a university degree to succeeding as a doctor or computer programmer or CEO, to raising kids who are competent and independent.

For Ayn Rand as for the Founding Fathers, abstract thought is not a game in which one cynically marvels at the alleged paradoxes of the universe. Thought—abstract thought—is purposeful. It demands a serious dedication to your life.

It demands the honesty of a mind seeking all the facts, because these and only these will dictate its conclusions about how to act. It demands the independence of a mind reaching its own verdict, no matter how many people say otherwise. It demands the integrity of a mind committed to acting on its own considered judgments. Thought is purposeful. Thought is selfish. Thought is for the sake of production.

The virtue of production, *Atlas Shrugged* shows, means a dedication to making the ideal real. It means far more than holding a job. It is a dedication to the work of "remaking the earth in the image of one's values." (*Atlas Shrugged*) It represents the proper union of the spiritual and the material. What the novel shows is that the souls of an artist and of an industrialist are the same.

The artist has a new vision of beauty, of what could be, and he strives to give it material form—to erect a sculpture of a woman, to paint a beautiful landscape, or to write *Cyrano de Bergerac*. The industrialist has a new vision of prosperity, of what could be, whether it be railroads crisscrossing the continent, a metal superior to steel, or a computer on every desk, and he works endlessly to bring it into existence. All production is born of a dedication to one's life in reality. It is the earthly form of idealism. Without it, there is no self-esteem.

A producer, in his dealings with other men, demands a non-sacrificial mode of existence. In issues of both matter and spirit, in money and in love, he is a *trader*.

> A trader does not ask to be paid for his failures, nor does he ask to be loved for his flaws. . . . Just as he does not give his work except in trade for material values, so he does not give the values of his spirit—his

love, his friendship, his esteem—except in payment and in trade for human virtues, in payment for his own selfish pleasure, which he receives from men he can respect. (*Atlas Shrugged*)

Notice how different this is from the Sermon on the Mount. And notice that on this approach trade is moral not because it achieves the welfare of the meek or the wealth of the nation. Trade's justification is not that it somehow commutes selfishness into selflessness. Adam Smith's invisible hand, taken as a justification, is corrupt.

Trade needs *no* outside justification. The justification of trade is precisely that it is a trade: it is an interaction in which *each* person is able to pursue his self-interest and happiness. It is the only form of interaction in which individuals meet one another as equals, not as exploiter and exploited. When you trade your paycheck for a new computer, both you and the seller are better off. You both obtain something more valuable to you than that which you gave up. Trade is the only form of human interaction that at once demands self-esteem—it demands that each trader be seeking the best for his own life—and, in turn, allows each person to preserve his self-esteem, because he has neither sacrificed his self to others, nor tried to cheat reality through the double standard of demanding the sacrifice of others to self.

Trade, production, and thought—these form the core of *Atlas Shrugged*'s new, life-based morality.

Notice how starkly this ideal contrasts to the Sermon on the Mount's religious conception of morality. Faith, hope, and charity are its virtues.

Faith means belief in the absence of logic. It is the opposite of thought.

Hope means that you are unable to reach the ideal, that perfection is beyond your reach, but that by God's grace you might obtain it, usually in some alleged afterlife. Hope is the opposite of working to create the ideal in this life. It is the opposite of production.

Charity means giving yourself over body and soul to your neighbor and even your enemy, with the expectation of no return. It is the opposite of trade.

Jesus on the cross exhibited these virtues. He had the faith that there was an other-worldly father. He had the hope that he would gain the grace of this other-worldly being. He had the charity to sacrifice his own soul for the redemption of sinners. The result was his death.

For a morality of life, this cannot be the image of the moral ideal. What then is? The great thinkers and producers. The scientists, philosophers, artists, inventors, and industrialists who make a human mode of existence possible—individuals like Aristotle, Newton, Edison and Rockefeller. Men such as these are the heroes of *Atlas Shrugged*.

Remember Jefferson's gallery of worthies? Who were some of the individuals included in it, other than himself? Philosophers like Francis Bacon and John Locke; scientists like Isaac Newton and Benjamin Franklin; political thinkers and men of action like Voltaire, Turgot, and Thomas Paine. In *Atlas Shrugged*'s terms, these are men of the mind.

And this gallery of worthies itself captures the greatness of America's founding: it was the possibility of such men and such achievements that served as the Revolution's deepest motive power. But the tragedy of the Revolution is that Jefferson and the other Founding Fathers still thought of Jesus as the sublime preacher of the Sermon on the Mount.

What *Atlas Shrugged* shows us is that the choice is *either-or*. And more: it shows us that Jefferson's gallery of worthies are worthy of that which they had never been granted before: *moral* respect, *moral* admiration, and *moral* esteem.

In *Atlas Shrugged*, the character of Hank Rearden is the representative of the man of self-esteem, of the true American. Rearden is an industrialist of tremendous intellect, drive, and productivity, who is denounced for his achievements. And although he possesses the core of self-esteem, he's hobbled by the thought that, morally, he's unworthy. *Atlas Shrugged* is the story of his liberation. To all such men of real self-esteem, the novel throws a lifeline from the morality of sacrifice. "They had known that theirs was the power. I taught them that theirs was the glory." (*Atlas Shrugged*)

Now you might be wondering, if *Atlas Shrugged* is chock full of new ideas, if it is America's second Declaration of Independence, why did Rand choose to first present her ideas in the form of a novel? Precisely because her concern was the moral *ideal*.

She wanted to give material expression to her new vision of the ideal. The form in which one does this is art. The goal of her writing, she said after *Atlas Shrugged*'s publication, "*is the projection of an ideal man.*" Art allows one to experience the ideal made real. It allows one to inhabit that world for a time. As anyone who has read *Atlas Shrugged* knows, the contemplation of a great work of art is an unforgettable and indispensable experience.

Rand of course knew that one can learn a lot from *Atlas Shrugged*. But she regarded this as a secondary benefit. The book's primary, essential value is that within its pages one experiences her new ideal made perceptible and real.

Any great, Romantic work of art is, to quote from one of her latter essays, "an entity complete in itself, an achieved, realized, immovable fact of reality—like a beacon raised over the dark crossroads of the world, saying: '*This* is possible.'"

This is what *Atlas Shrugged* does for us.

But to now make real in our own lives the ideal presented in *Atlas Shrugged*, and to restore America to her greatness as the country dedicated to the individual and his happiness, we must be willing to challenge moral ideas inculcated since childhood. We must realize that one of the most difficult feats is to question our existing moral views and embrace a radically new moral code; nothing less will do. To reverse the trend toward Big Government, to halt the transfer of power from the hands of the individual to the hands of the state, we must become uncompromising champions of the individual. And we must do so not because the world might go to hell in thirty or forty years if we don't. Although it might, that's not the issue. The Founding Fathers did not create a new nation because their world was about to go to hell; they created a new nation to achieve the ideal.

But to champion the individual's moral right to his life, to his liberty of thought and action, to his selfish pursuit of property and happiness, we must be willing to challenge the Sermon on the Mount. In the name of our own self-esteem, we must proudly say "No" to a moral doctrine that chains the individual to other people, that demands that one feel guilty for success, and that divides mankind into servants and masters. We must instead embrace a code that extols the virtues of thought, production, and trade and declares that the purpose of morality is to teach you how to achieve your own life and happiness. We must recognize that a moral code of individualism is the only code compatible with America's uniqueness.

Rand's *Atlas Shrugged is* America's second Declaration of Independence. But what remains for us to do is to pledge our lives, our fortunes, and our sacred honor to understanding and realizing its vision of the ideal.

Based on a 2007 talk, this essay previously appeared in New Ideal *on September 17, 2018.*

ENDNOTES

Profit Without Apology: The Need to Stand Up for Business

1. Ayn Rand, "The Moratorium on Brains," *The Ayn Rand Letter* (Santa Ana, CA: Ayn Rand Institute Press, 2024), 5–14.

2. Angus Deaton, *The Great Escape* (Princeton, NJ: Princeton University Press, 2013), 128.

3. Steven Pinker, *Enlightenment Now* (New York: Viking, 2018), 176–185.

4. Alex Epstein, *Fossil Future* (New York: Portfolio, 2022), 258–84.

5. Deirdre McCloskey, *Bourgeois Dignity* (Chicago: University of Chicago Press, 2010), 55–56.

6. Ayn Rand, *For the New Intellectual* (New York: Signet, 1961), 27.

7. Marc Benioff, "Marc Benioff: We Need a New Capitalism," *New York Times*, October 14, 2019, at https://www.nytimes.com/2019/10/14/opinion/benioff-salesforce-capitalism.html.

8. Evie Fordham, "AOC: 'No one ever makes a billion dollars. You take a billion dollars,'" *Fox Business*, January 21, 2020, at https://www.foxbusiness.com/money/aoc-billionaires-ta-nehisi-coates-interview.

9. See, for instance, Don Watkins, "The Great Depression and the Role of Government Intervention," Ayn Rand Institute, February 1, 2017, at https://ari.aynrand.org/

the-great-depression-and-the-role-of-government-intervention/.; Onkar Ghate, "No Right to 'Free' Health Care," Ayn Rand Institute, June 11, 2007, at https://ari.aynrand.org/issues/government-and-business/healthcare/no-right-to-free-health-care/.; Don Watkins, "Free Markets Didn't Create the Great Recession," Ayn Rand Institute, March 1, 2017, at https://ari.aynrand.org/free-markets-didnt-create-the-great-recession/.

10. Jim Zarroli, "Visiting New York City, Bernie Sanders Attacks Clinton, 'Greed' Of Wall Street." *NPR*, January 6, 2016, at https://www.npr.org/2016/01/06/462094414/visiting-new-york-city-bernie-sanders-attacks-clinton-greed-of-wall-street.

11. The Atlas Circle, "Open Letter to Sundar Pichai and the Google Team," *The Atlas Circle* (Substack), January 29, 2025, at https://theatlascircle.substack.com/p/open-letter-to-sundar-pichai-and.

12. Irving Kristol, *Two Cheers for Capitalism* (New York: Basic Books, 1978), 80.

13. Martin Luther King, Jr., *Where Do We Go from Here: Chaos or Community?* (Boston: Beacon Press, 1967), 197.

14. Mark Felsenthal, "Greenspan 'Schocked' at Credit Breakdown," *Reuters*, October 23, 2008, at https://www.reuters.com/article/uk-financial-greenspan-idUKTRE49M5SJ20081023/.

15. Thomas Sowell, *Barbarians inside the Gates and Other Controversial Essays* (Stanford, CA: Hoover Institution Press, 1999), 250.

16. Ayn Rand, *For the New Intellectual*, 144.

17. Ayn Rand, *For the New Intellectual*, 123.

18. For an overview of this moral theory, see Ayn Rand, "The Objectivist Ethics," In *The Virtue of Selfishness: A New Concept of Egoism* (New York: Signet, 1964), 13–39.

19. Onkar Ghate, "Freedom and the Need for Business to Stand Up for Itself," Ayn Rand Institute, YouTube video, 1:20:36, July 17, 2014, at https://www.youtube.com/watch?v=ZT5VRn5P1D8.

Open Letter to Sundar Pichai and the Google Team

1. Kent Walker, "DOJ's staggering proposal would hurt consumers and America's global technological leadership," *The Keyword* (November 21, 2024), at https://blog.google/outreach-initiatives/public-policy/doj-search-remedies-nov-2024/.

2. D. Michaels and M. Kruppa, "Google Should Be Forced to Sell Chrome Browser, Justice Department Says," *Wall Street Journal* (November 21, 2024). At https://www.wsj.com/tech/google-should-be-forced-to-sell-chrome-browser-justice-department-says-13602df9?mod=hp_lead_pos1

3. S. Vranica and M. Kruppa, "Google's Grip on Search Slips as TikTok and AI Startup Mount Challenge," *Wall Street Journal* (October 5, 2024). At https://www.wsj.com/tech/online-ad-market-google-tiktok-9599d7e8.

4. *US v. Google*, Judge Mehta ruling (August 5, 2024). At https://www.documentcloud.org/documents/25032745-045110819896/.

5. *Ibid*.

6. Lee-Anne Mulholland, "Our remedies proposal in DOJ's search distribution case," *The Keyword* (December, 2024.) At https://blog.google/outreach-initiatives/public-policy/google-remedies-proposal-dec-2024/.

7. Ayn Rand, "Antitrust: The Rule of Unreason," in *The Objectivist Newsletter: 1962–1965* (Santa Ana, CA: Ayn Rand Institute Press, 2024), 5.

8. Ayn Rand, "America's Persecuted Minority: Big Business," in *Capitalism: The Unknown Ideal* (New York: Signet, 1967), 44–62.

Standing Up to DEI Activism: A Guide for Executives

1. Maxine Williams, "2019 Diversity Report," Meta, July 9, 2019, at https://about.fb.com/news/2019/07/2019-diversity-report/.

2. Kari Paul, "Facebook Accused of Systemic Racial Bias in Hiring," *The Guardian*, March 5, 2021, at https://www.theguardian.com/technology/2021/mar/05/facebook-systemic-racial-bias-hiring-eeoc-investigation.

3. The Conference Board, *C-Suite Challenge*™ 2020: Creating a Future-Ready Organization, 2020, at http://www.conference-board.org/publications/C-Suite-Challenge-2020.

4. Shereen Daniels, *The Anti-Racist Organization: Dismantling Systemic Racism in the Workplace* (Hoboken, NJ: Wiley, 2022), 33.

5. Ibram X. Kendi, *How to Be an Antiracist* (New York: One World, 2019), 21.

6. Ibram X. Kendi, *How to Be an Antiracist*, 22.

7. Daniel Bergner, "The White Fragility Debate," *The New York Times Magazine*, July 15, 2020, at https://www.nytimes.com/2020/07/15/magazine/white-fragility-robin-diangelo.html.

8. Kim T. Wilson, *Diversity, Equity, and Inclusion in the Workplace* (New York: HarperCollins Leadership, 2022), 14.

9. Shereen Daniels, *The Anti-Racist Organization*, 103.

10. Mary-Frances Winters, *Racial Justice at Work: Practical Solutions for Systemic Change* (San Francisco: Berrett-Koehler Publishers, 2023), 2.

11. Mary-Fances Winters, *Racial Justice at Work*, 3.

12. Ibram X. Kendi, *How to Be an Antiracist*, 181.

13. Ibram X. Kendi, *How to Be an Antiracist*, 176.

14. Shereen Daniels, *The Anti-Racist Organization*, 28.

15. Robin DiAngelo, "Anti-Racism: A One-Page Handout, 2016," at https://robindiangelo.com/wp-content/uploads/2016/06/Anti-racism-handout-1-page-2016.pdf.

16. William A. Jacobson, "The Battle over Diversity Training," Cato Institute, November 2, 2020, at https://www.cato.org/commentary/battle-over-diversity-training.

17. Jena McGregor, "To Improve Diversity, Don't Make People Go to Diversity Training. Really," *The Washington Post*, July 1, 2016, at https://www.washingtonpost.com/news/on-leadership/wp/2016/07/01/to-improve-diversity-dont-make-people-go-to-diversity-training-really-2/.

18. Ayn Rand, "Compromise," in *The Ayn Rand Lexicon: Objectivism from A to Z*, edited by Harry Binswanger (New York: Meridian, 1986), 87–88.

19. Chris Marr, "Host of Companies Sued Alleging Unmet Diversity, Equity Pledges," *Bloomberg Law*, August 16, 2023, at https://news.bloomberglaw.com/esg/host-of-companies-sued-alleging-unmet-diversity-equity-pledges.

20. This article cites two, though we cannot endorse any particular training program.

21. John Sailer, "How DEI Is Supplanting Truth as the Mission of American Universities," *The Free Press*, January 9, 2023, at https://www.thefp.com/p/how-dei-is-supplanting-truth-as-the.

22. Don Watkins, "More University Donors Should 'Go Galt,'" *New Ideal*, April 24, 2023, at https://newideal.aynrand.org/more-university-donors-should-go-galt/.

23. Pierce Gentry, "UT System to Rename Division of Diversity and Engagement as Access and Engagement," *The Daily Beacon*, November 14, 2023, at https://www.utdailybeacon.com/campus_news/administration/ut-system-to-rename-division-of-diversity-and-engagement-as-access-and-engagement/article_216bffec-835e-11ee-8b3f-938598cc8b8c.html.

ABOUT THE CONTRIBUTORS

Onkar Ghate is chief philosophy officer and a senior fellow at the Ayn Rand Institute. He is the Institute's resident expert on Objectivism and serves as its senior trainer and editor.

Don Watkins is vice president of fundraising and marketing at the Ayn Rand Institute. He is the best-selling author of books such as *Free Market Revolution* (co-authored with Yaron Brook) and, most recently, *Effective Egoism*.

Robert Bakula is an associate fellow and intellectual incubator operations specialist at the Ayn Rand Institute; he writes and speaks for ARI, and he is a teaching assistant at the ARI's' educational programs.

Elan Journo is a senior fellow and vice president at the Ayn Rand Institute. His books include *What Justice Demands: America and the Israeli-Palestinian Conflict*, *Failing to Confront Islamic Totalitarianism: What Went Wrong after 9/11*, and *Illuminating Ayn Rand*.

Tal Tsfany is the president and CEO of the Ayn Rand Institute. He has been an entrepreneur, investor and executive in the software world. He is a co-founder of the Ayn Rand Center Israel.

ABOUT THE AYN RAND INSTITUTE

The Ayn Rand Institute fosters a growing awareness, understanding and acceptance of Ayn Rand's philosophy, Objectivism, in order to create a culture whose guiding principles are reason, rational self-interest, individualism and laissez-faire capitalism—a culture in which individuals are free to pursue their own happiness.

ABOUT THE ATLAS CIRCLE

The Atlas Circle is an initiative of the Ayn Rand Institute created to stand up for business—and to empower business leaders to stand up for themselves.

atlascircle.org

ABOUT ARU PRESS

The Institute's ARU venture is the premier place worldwide for education in the philosophy of Objectivism and its applications. ARU Press publishes works by faculty and affiliated scholars, including writings from ARI's journal *New Ideal*.

Made in the USA
Columbia, SC
10 July 2025